KETO RE(
BUDGET

The Ultimate Collection of Succulent and
Healthy Low-Carb Recipes for Smart
People on a Budget

Written by

Sam Gallo

Table of Contents

Introduction

Want to follow a ketogenic diet but not sure where to start? Struggling with finding delicious and tummy-filling recipes when going "against the grains"? Do not worry! In this book you will find mouth-watering delights for any occasion and any eater, you will not believe that these recipes will help you restore your health and slim down your body.

Successfully practiced for more than nine decades, the ketogenic diet hs proven to be the ultimate long-term diet for any person. The restriction list may frighten many, but the truth is, this diet is super adaptable, and the food combinations and tasty meals are pretty endless.

Most people believe that our bodies are designed to run on carbohydrates. We think that ingesting carbohydrates is the only way to provide our bodies with the energy they need to function normally. However, what many people don't know is that carbohydrates are not the only source of fuel our bodies can use. Our bodies can also use fat as an energy source! When we decide to ditch carbs and provide our bodies with more fat, then we've begun our journey into the ketogenic diet, and this cookbook will be the guide you need to make your journey simple and enjoyable...let's start!

Breakfast recipes

Frittata with Spinach & Ricotta

Ingredients for 4 servings

1 cup spinach
8 oz crumbled ricotta cheese
1 pint halved cherry tomatoes
10 eggs
3 tbsp olive oil
4 green onions, diced

Directions and Total Time: approx. 40 minutes

Preheat oven to 350 F. In a bowl, whisk the eggs. Stir in spinach, ricotta cheese, and green onions. Pour the mixture into a greased casserole, top with cherry tomatoes, and bake for 25 minutes. Cut in wedges and serve.

Per serving: Cal 461; Net Carbs: 6g; Fat: 35g; Protein: 26g

Herby Paprika Biscuits

Ingredients for 4 servings

1 cup almond flour
1/8 cup melted butter
1 egg
½ tsp salt
¼ tsp black pepper
¼ tsp garlic powder
½ tsp baking soda
½ tsp paprika powder
½ tbsp plain vinegar
½ cup mixed dried herbs

Directions and Total Time: approx. 30 minutes

Preheat oven to 350 F. Line a baking sheet with parchment paper. In a food processor, mix flour, melted butter, egg, salt, pepper, garlic powder, baking soda, paprika, vinegar, and dried herbs until smoothly combined. Mold 12 balls out of the mixture and arrange on the baking sheet at 2-inch intervals. Bake for 25 minutes or until golden brown.

Per serving: Cal 73; Net Carbs 0.6g, Fat 7.2g, Protein 1.6g

Raspberry Almond Smoothie

Ingredients for 4 servings

1 ½ cups almond milk
½ cup raspberries
Juice from half lemon
½ tsp almond extract

Directions and Total Time: approx. 5 minutes

In a blender or smoothie maker, pour the almond milk, raspberries, lemon juice, and almond extract.

Puree the ingredients on high speed until the raspberries have blended almost entirely into the liquid. Serve.

Per serving: Cal 406; Net Carbs 9g; Fat 38g; Protein 5g

Strawberry Donuts

Ingredients for 4 servings

For the donuts:
½ cup butter
2 oz cream cheese
¼ cup sour cream
1 ½ tsp vanilla extract
½ cup erythritol
10 fresh strawberries, mashed
2 tsp lemon juice
2 tsp water
2 egg whites
2 cups blanched almond flour
2 tbsp protein powder
2 tsp baking powder

For the glaze:
4 fresh strawberries, mashed
2 tbsp coconut cream
2 tbsp xylitol
2 tsp water

Directions and Total Time: approx. 25 minutes

Preheat oven to 350 F. For the donuts, in a bowl, whisk butter, cream cheese, sour cream, vanilla, erythritol, strawberries, lemon juice, water, and egg whites until smooth. In another bowl, mix almond flour, protein and baking powders. Combine both mixtures until smooth. Pour the batter into greased donut cups and bake for 15 minutes. Flip the donuts onto a wire rack to cool.

In a bowl, combine strawberries, coconut cream, xylitol, and water until smooth. Swirl the glaze over the donuts.

Per serving: Cal 320; Net Carbs 5.9g, Fat 32g, Protein 4.2g

Coconut Waffles with Cranberries

Ingredients for 4 servings

6 tbsp unsalted butter, melted and cooled slightly
2/3 cup coconut flour
2 ½ tsp baking powder
A pinch of salt
2 eggs
1 ½ cups almond milk
Greek yogurt for topping
¼ cup fresh cranberries
2/3 cup erythritol
1 tsp lemon zest
½ tsp vanilla extract

Directions and Total Time: approx. 16 minutes

Add cranberries, erythritol, 3/4 cup water, vanilla, and lemon zest in a saucepan. Bring to a boil and reduce the temperature; simmer for 15 minutes or until the cranberries break and a sauce forms; set aside. In a bowl, mix coconut flour, baking powder, and salt. In another bowl, whisk eggs, almond milk, and butter and pour the mixture into the flour mixture. Combine until a smooth batter forms. Preheat a waffle iron and brush with butter. Pour some of the batter and cook until golden and crisp, 4 minutes. Repeat with the remaining batter. Plate the waffles, spoon a dollop of yogurt on top followed by the cranberry sauce.

Per serving: Cal 247; Net Carbs 6.9g; Fat 21g; Protein 6.6g

Creamy Salmon Tortilla Wraps

Ingredients for 4 servings

4 tbsp cottage cheese
1 lime, zested and juiced
2 tsp chopped fresh dill
Salt and black pepper to taste
4 (7-inch) low carb tortillas
8 slices smoked salmon

Directions and Total Time: approx. 10 min + chilling time

In a bowl, mix cottage cheese, lime juice, zest, dill, salt, and black pepper. Lay each tortilla on a plastic wrap (just wide enough to cover the tortilla), spread with cottage cheese mixture, and top each (one) with two salmon slices. Roll up the tortillas and secure both ends by twisting. Refrigerate for 2 hours, remove plastic, cut off both ends of each wrap, and cut wraps into half-inch wheels.

Per serving: Cal 250; Net Carbs 7g; Fat 16g; Protein 18g

Mascarpone Cheese Cups Cheese Cups

Ingredients for 4 servings

1 cup mascarpone cheese
4 tbsp olive oil
2 cups almond flour
2 tsp baking soda
1 egg
1 cup almond milk

Directions and Total Time: approx. 30 minutes

Preheat oven to 380 F. Grease a muffin tray with cooking spray. In a bowl, mix almond flour and baking soda. In a separate bowl, beat mascarpone cheese and olive oil and whisk in egg and almond milk. Fold in flour and spoon 2 tbsp of the batter into each muffin cup. Bake for 20 minutes, remove to a wire rack, and cool. Serve.

Per serving: Cal 299; Net Carbs 3.2g; Fat 26g; Protein 11g

Croque Madame with Pesto

Ingredients for 4 servings

1 (7-oz) can sliced mushrooms, drained
4 tbsp melted butter
1 cup almond milk
2 tbsp almond flour
Salt and black pepper to taste
½ tsp nutmeg powder
4 tbsp grated Monterey Jack
½ cup basil leaves
1/3 cup toasted pine nuts
¼ cup grated Parmesan
1 garlic clove, peeled
¼ cup + 1 tbsp olive oil
4 slices zero carb bread
3 medium tomatoes, sliced
4 slices mozzarella cheese
4 large whole eggs
Baby arugula for garnishing

Directions and Total Time: approx. 45 minutes

To make bechamel sauce, place half of the butter and half of the milk in a saucepan over medium heat. Whisk in the remaining milk with flour until smooth roux forms. Season with salt, pepper, and nutmeg. Reduce the heat and stir in Monterey Jack cheese until melted. Set aside the bechamel sauce. For the pesto, in a food processor, puree basil, pine nuts, Parmesan cheese, garlic, and ¼ cup olive oil. Refrigerate the resulting pesto in a glass jar. Preheat grill to medium-high. Brush both sides of each bread slice with remaining butter.

Toast each on both sides. Remove onto a plate and spread béchamel sauce on one side of each bread, then pesto, and top with tomatoes and mozzarella cheese. One after the other, return each sandwich to the grill and cook until the cheese melts. Heat the remaining olive oil in a skillet and crack in eggs. Cook until the whites set but the yolks still soft and runny. Place the eggs on the sandwiches. Garnish with arugula.

Per serving: Cal 630; Net Carbs 3.7g; Fat 55g; Protein 25g

Starter and Salad

Classic Greek Salad

Ingredients for 4 servings

5 tomatoes, chopped
1 cucumber, chopped
1 green bell pepper, chopped
1 small red onion, chopped
16 kalamata olives, chopped
4 tbsp capers
7 oz feta cheese, chopped
1 tsp oregano, dried
4 tbsp olive oil
Salt to taste

Directions and Total Time: approx. 10 minutes

Place tomatoes, bell pepper, cucumber, onion, feta cheese, and olives in a bowl. Mix to combine well. Season with salt. Combine the capers, olive oil, and oregano in a small bowl. Drizzle the dressing over the salad and serve.

Per serving: Cal 323; Net Carbs 8g; Fat 28g; Protein 9.3g

Mayo & Broccoli Slaw

Ingredients for 6 servings

2 tbsp swerve
1 tbsp Dijon mustard
1 tbsp olive oil
4 cups broccoli slaw
⅓ cup mayonnaise
1 tsp celery seeds
1 ½ tbsp apple cider vinegar
Salt and black pepper to taste

Directions and Total Time: approx. 10 minutes

Whisk together all ingredients, except for broccoli. Place broccoli in a large salad bowl. Pour the dressing over. Mix to combine and serve.

Per serving: Cal 110; Net Carbs 2g; Fat 10g; Protein 3g

Roasted Mushrooms with Green Beans

Ingredients for 4 servings

1 lb cremini mushrooms, sliced
4 tbsp hazelnuts, chopped
½ lb green beans
3 tbsp melted butter
Juice of 1 lemon

Directions and Total Time: approx. 25 minutes

Preheat oven to 450 F. Arrange mushrooms and green beans in a baking dish and drizzle with butter. Roast for 20 minutes. Transfer to a bowl, drizzle with lemon juice and toss with hazelnuts. Serve.

Per serving: Cal 179; Net Carbs 7g; Fat 11g; Protein 5g

Squash Salad

Ingredients for 4 servings

1 fennel bulb, sliced
2 lb green squash, cubed
2 tbsp butter
2 oz chopped green onions
1 cup mayonnaise
2 tbsp chives, finely chopped
A pinch of mustard powder
2 tbsp chopped dill

Directions and Total Time: approx. 20 minutes

Put a pan over medium heat and melt butter. Fry squash until slightly softened, about 7 minutes; let cool. In a bowl, mix squash, fennel slices, green onions, mayonnaise, chives, and mustard powder. Garnish with dill and serve.

Per serving: Cal 317; Net Carbs 3g; Fat 31g; Protein 4g

Beet Tofu Salad

Ingredients for 4 servings

8 oz red beets, washed
2 oz tofu, cubed
2 tbsp butter
½ red onion, sliced
1 cup mayonnaise
1 small romaine lettuce, torn
Salt and black pepper to taste
Freshly chopped chives

Directions and Total Time: approx. 10 55

Put beets in a pot over medium heat, cover with salted water and bring to a boil for 40 minutes or until soft. Drainand allow cooling. Slip the skin off and slice the beets. Melt butter in a g pan over medium heat and fry tofu until browned, 3-4 minutes. Remove to a plate. In a salad bowl, combine beets, tofu, red onion, lettuce, salt, pepper, and mayonnaise. Garnish with chives and serve.

Per serving: Cal 415; Net Carbs 2g; Fat 40g; Protein 7g

Warm Collard Green Salad

Ingredients for 2 servings

¾ cup coconut cream
2 tbsp mayonnaise
1 tsp mustard powder
2 tbsp coconut oil
1 garlic clove, minced
1 tbsp butter
1 cup collard greens, rinsed
4 oz tofu cheese

Directions and Total Time: approx. 10 minutes

In a bowl, whisk whipping cream, mayonnaise, mustard powder, coconut oil, garlic, salt, and pepper until well mixed; set aside. Melt butter in a skillet over medium heat and sauté collard greens until wilted and brownish. Transfer to a salad bowl and pour the creamy dressing over. Mix the salad well and crumble the tofu cheese over.

Per serving: Cal 495; Net Carbs 5g; Fat 46g; Protein 11g

Soup and stews

Spring Vegetable Soup

Ingredients for 4 servings

4 cups vegetable stock
1 cup pearl onions, halved
3 cups green beans, chopped
2 cups asparagus, chopped
2 cups baby spinach
1 tbsp garlic powder
Salt and white pepper to taste
2 cups grated Parmesan

Directions and Total Time: approx. 25 minutes

Pour vegetable broth into a pot over medium heat and add pearl onions, green beans, and asparagus. Season with garlic powder, salt and white pepper and cook for 10 minutes. Stir in spinach and allow slight wilting. Top with Parmesan cheese and serve.

Per serving: Cal 196; Net Carbs 4.3g; Fat 12g, Protein 2.5g

Chilled Lemongrass & Avocado Soup

Ingredients for 4 servings

4 cups chopped avocado pulp
2 stalks lemongrass, chopped
4 cups vegetable broth
2 lemons, juiced
3 tbsp chopped mint
2 cups heavy cream

Directions and Total Time: approx. 20 min + chilling time

Bring avocado, lemongrass, and vegetable broth to a boil in a pot over low heat for 10 minutes. Remove from the heat, add in lemon juice, and puree the ingredients using an immersion blender. Stir in heavy cream. Spoon into bowls and chill for 1 hour. Garnish with mint and serve.

Per serving: Cal 339; Net Carbs 3.5g; Fat 33g, Protein 3.5g

Wild Mushroom Soup

Ingredients for 4 servings

12 oz wild mushrooms, chopped
¼ cup butter
5 oz crème fraiche
2 tsp fresh thyme, chopped
2 garlic cloves, minced
4 cups chicken broth
Salt and black pepper to taste

Directions and Total Time: approx. 30 minutes

Melt butter in a large pot over medium heat. Add and sauté garlic for 1 minute until tender. Add in wild mushrooms, season with salt and pepper, and cook for 5 minutes. Pour the chicken broth over and bring to a boil. Reduce the heat and simmer for 10 minutes. Blitz with a hand blender until smooth. Stir in crème fraiche. Serve topped with thyme.

Per serving: Cal 281; Net Carbs 5.8g; Fat 25g, Protein 6g

Creamy Feta Soup

Ingredients for 4 servings

1 cup cremini mushrooms, sliced and pre-cooked
1 tbsp olive oil
1 garlic clove, minced
1 white onion, finely chopped
1 tsp ginger puree
1 cup vegetable stock
2 turnips, peeled and chopped
Salt and black pepper to taste
1 cup feta cheese, crumbled
2 cups almond milk
1 tbsp chopped basil
Finely chopped parsley
Chopped walnuts for topping

Directions and Total Time: approx. 25 minutes

Heat olive oil in a saucepan over medium heat and sauté garlic, onion, and ginger puree until fragrant and soft, about 3 minutes. Pour in vegetable stock, turnips and season with salt and pepper; cook for 6 minutes. Use an immersion blender to puree the ingredients until smooth. Stir in mushrooms and simmer covered for 7 minutes. Add in almond milk and heat for 2 minutes. Stir in basil and parsley and sprinkle with feta cheese. Serve warm.

Per serving: Cal 923; Net Carbs 7.4g; Fat 8.5g, Protein 23g

Cauliflower Soup with Kielbasa

Ingredients for 4 servings

1 cauliflower head, chopped
1 rutabaga, chopped
3 tbsp ghee
1 kielbasa sausage, sliced
2 cups chicken broth
1 small onion, chopped
2 cups water
Salt and black pepper, to taste

Directions and Total Time: approx. 35 minutes

Melt the ghee in a pot over medium heat and cook kielbasa sausage for 5 minutes; reserve. Add onion to the pot and sauté for 3 minutes. Add in cauliflower and rutabaga and cook for another 5 minutes. Pour in broth, water, salt, and pepper. Bring to a boil and simmer for 15 minutes. Puree the soup until smooth. Serve topped with kielbasa.

Per serving: Cal 251; Net Carbs: 5g; Fat: 19g, Protein: 10g

Lunch and dinner

Spanish Paella "Keto-Style"

Ingredients for 4 servings

½ pound rabbit, cut into pieces
½ pound chicken drumsticks
1 white onion, chopped
2 garlic cloves, minced
1 red bell pepper, chopped
2 tbsp olive oil
½ cup thyme, chopped
1 tsp smoked paprika
2 tbsp tomato puree
½ cup white wine
1 cup chicken broth
2 cups cauli rice
1 cup green beans, chopped
A pinch of saffron

Directions and Total Time: approx. 70 minutes

Preheat oven to 350 F. Warm olive oil in a pan. Fry chicken and rabbit on all sides for 8 minutes; remove to a plate. Add onion and garlic to the pan and sauté for 3 minutes. Include in tomato puree, bell pepper, and smoked paprika and let simmer for 2 minutes. Pour in broth and simmer for 6 minutes. Stir in cauli rice, white wine, green beans, saffron, and thyme and lay the meat on top. Transfer the pan to the oven and cook for 20 minutes. Season and serve.

Per serving: Cal 378; Net Carbs 7.6g; Fat 21g; Protein 37g

Smothered Chicken Breasts with Bacon

Ingredients for 6 servings

7 strips bacon, chopped
3 chicken breasts, halved
Salt and black pepper to taste
5 sprigs fresh thyme
¼ cup chicken broth
½ cup heavy cream

Directions and Total Time: approx. 25 minutes

Cook bacon in a skillet for 5 minutes; remove to a plate. Season chicken breasts with salt and pepper and brown in the bacon fat for 4 minutes on each side. Remove to the bacon plate. Stir thyme, chicken broth, and heavy cream in the skillet and simmer for 5 minutes. Return the chicken and bacon and cook for 2 minutes. Serve warm.

Per serving: Cal 435; Net Carbs 3g; Fat 37g; Protein 22g

Baked Spicy Cauliflower & Peppers

Ingredients for 4 servings

1 lb cauliflower, cut into florets
1 yellow bell pepper, halved
1 red bell pepper, halved
¼ cup olive oil
Salt and black pepper, to taste
½ tsp cayenne pepper
1 tsp curry powder

Directions and Total Time: approx. 35 minutes

Preheat oven to 425 F. Line a parchment paper to a baking sheet. Sprinkle olive oil to the peppers and cauliflower alongside curry powder, pepper, salt, and cayenne pepper. Set the vegetables on the baking sheet. Roast for 30 minutes as you toss in intervals until they start to brown. Serve alongside mushroom pate or homemade tomato dip.

Per serving: Cal 166; Net Carbs: 7g; Fat: 14g; Protein: 3g

Spanish Broccoli Gratin

Ingredients for 4 servings

1 head broccoli, broken into florets
1 cup Manchego cheese, grated
2 tbsp olive oil
1 garlic clove, minced
1 rosemary sprig, chopped
1 thyme sprig, chopped

Directions and Total Time: approx. 15 minutes

Add broccoli in boiling salted water over medium heat and cook for 8 minutes. Remove to a casserole dish and mix in olive oil, garlic, rosemary, and thyme. Scatter the cheese all over. Preheat oven to 380 F. Insert the casserole and bake for 10 minutes until the cheese is melted. Serve.

Per serving: Cal 230; Net Carbs: 7g; Fat: 17g; Protein: 12g

Spinach with Garlic & Thyme

Ingredients for 4 servings

½ tsp red pepper flakes, crushed
2 pound spinach, chopped
2 tbsp almond oil
1 tsp garlic, minced
½ tsp thyme

Directions and Total Time: approx. 25 minutes

Add spinach in a pot with salted water over medium heat and cook for 3 minutes. Drain and set aside. Place a sauté pan over medium heat and warm the almond oil. Cook in garlic until soft, 1 minute. Stir in spinach, red pepper flakes, and thyme for 2 minutes. Serve warm.

Per serving: Cal 118; Net Carbs: 13g; Fat: 7g; Protein: 3g

Hazelnut & Cheese Stuffed Zucchinis

Ingredients for 4 servings

2 tbsp olive oil
1 cup cauliflower rice
¼ cup vegetable broth
1 ¼ cup diced tomatoes
1 red onion, chopped
¼ cup pine nuts
¼ cup hazelnuts
4 tbsp chopped cilantro
1 tbsp balsamic vinegar
1 tbsp smoked paprika
2 medium zucchinis, halved
1 cup grated Monterey Jack

Directions and Total Time: approx. 35 minutes

Preheat oven to 350 F. Pour cauli rice and broth in a pot and cook for 5 minutes. Fluff the cauli rice and allow cooling. Scoop the flesh out of the zucchini halves using a spoon and chop the pulp. Brush the zucchini shells with some olive oil. In a bowl, mix cauli rice, tomatoes, red onion, pine nuts, hazelnuts, cilantro, vinegar, paprika, and zucchini pulp. Spoon the mixture into the zucchini halves, drizzle with remaining olive oil, and sprinkle the cheese on top. Bake for 20 minutes until the cheese melts. Serve.

Per serving: Cal 330; Net Carbs 5.2g; Fat 28g; Protein 12g

Herby Mushroom Stroganoff

Ingredients for 4 servings

½ cup grated Pecorino Romano cheese
3 tbsp butter
1 white onion, chopped
4 cups mushrooms, chopped
½ cup heavy cream
1 ½ tbsp dried mixed herbs
Salt and black pepper to taste

Directions and Total Time: approx. 15 minutes

Melt butter in a saucepan and sauté onion for 3 minutes. Stir in mushrooms and cook for 3 minutes. Add 2 cups water and bring to boil; cook for 4 minutes. Pour in heavy cream and Pecorino Romano cheese. Stir to melt the cheese. Also, mix in dried herbs. Season with salt and pepper. Ladle stroganoff over spaghetti squash and serve.

Per serving: Cal 284; Net Carbs 1.5g; Fat 28g; Protein 8g

Avocado Carbonara

Ingredients for 4 servings

8 tbsp flax seed powder
1 ½ cups cream cheese
5 ½ tbsp psyllium husk
1 avocado, peeled and pitted
1 ¾ cups coconut cream
Juice of ½ lemon
1 teaspoon onion powder
½ teaspoon garlic powder
¼ cup olive oil
Salt and black pepper to taste
¼ cup grated Parmesan
4 tbsp toasted pecans

Directions and Total Time: approx. 30 minutes

Preheat oven to 300 F. In a bowl, mix flax seed powder with 1 ½ cups water and let sit to thicken for 5 minutes. Add cream cheese, 1 tsp salt, and psyllium husk. Whisk until smooth batter forms. Line a baking sheet with parchment paper, pour in the batter and cover with another parchment paper. Use a rolling pin to flatten the dough into the sheet. Bake for 12 minutes. Remove, take off the parchment papers and slice the "pasta" into thin strips lengthwise.

Cut each piece into halves, pour into a bowl, and set aside. In a blender, combine avocado, coconut cream, lemon juice, onion and garlic powders and puree until smooth. Pour olive oil over the pasta and stir to coat. Pour avocado sauce on top and mix. Sprinkle with salt, pepper, and Parmesan. Plate the pasta, garnish with pecans, and serve.

Per serving: Cal 870; Net Carbs 8g; Fat 69g; Protein 35g

Hazelnut Tofu Stir-Fry

Ingredients for 4 servings

1 tbsp tomato paste with garlic and onion
1 tbsp olive oil
1 (8 oz) firm tofu, cubed
1 tbsp balsamic vinegar
Salt and black pepper to taste
½ tsp mixed dried herbs
1 cup chopped raw hazelnuts

Directions and Total Time: approx. 15 minutes

Heat oil in a skillet and cook tofu for 3 minutes. In a bowl, mix tomato paste with the balsamic vinegar and add to the tofu. Stir, season with salt and black pepper, and cook for another 4 minutes. Add the herbs and hazelnuts. Stir and cook on low heat for 3 minutes until fragrant. Spoon to a side of squash mash and a sweet berry sauce to serve.

Per serving: Cal 320; Net Carbs 4g; Fat 24g; Protein 18g

Poultry

Harissa Chicken Tenders

Ingredients for 4 servings

1 tbsp harissa paste
1 tsp garlic powder
1 tsp smoked paprika
4 lemon wedges
2 eggs
3 tbsp butter, melted
½ cup white wine
1 lb chicken tenders
2 tbsp fresh mint, chopped
Salt and black pepper to taste

Directions and Total Time: approx. 45 min + chilling time

In a large bowl, combine butter, harissa, garlic powder, paprika, salt and pepper. Add in the chicken and mix well to coat. Cover with plastic wrap and refrigerate for 1 hour.

Preheat oven to 360 F. Remove the chicken and transfer to a greased baking dish. Add in the white wine and ½ cup water. Bake until the chicken is well done, about 20-25 minutes. Serve topped with mint and lemon wedges.

Per serving: Cal 354, Net Carbs 0.8g, Fat 19g, Protein 36g

Thyme Zucchini & Chicken Skillet

Ingredients for 4 servings

2 tbsp olive oil
1 tbsp unsalted butter
1 lb chicken chunks
1 finely chopped onion
¼ cup chopped fresh parsley
3 zucchinis, cut into 1-inch dices
1 tsp dried thyme
Salt and black pepper to taste

Directions and Total Time: approx. 30 minutes

Heat olive oil and butter in a skillet over medium heat and sauté chicken for 5 minutes. Add in onion and parsley and cook further for 3 minutes. Stir in zucchini and thyme, season with salt and pepper, cover, and cook for 8-10 minutes or until the vegetables soften. Serve immediately.

Per serving: Cal 157; Net Carbs 0.2g; Fat 12g; Protein 8g

Roasted Chicken with Yogurt Scallions Sauce

Ingredients for 4 servings

2 tbsp butter
4 scallions, chopped
4 chicken breasts
Salt and black pepper, to taste
6 ounces plain yogurt
2 tbsp fresh dill, chopped

Directions and Total Time: approx. 35 minutes

Melt butter in a pan, add in chicken, season with pepper and salt, and fry for 2-3 per side. Transfer to a greased baking dish and bake for 15 minutes at 390 F.

To the pan, add scallions and cook for 2 minutes. Pour in yogurt, warm without boil. Slice the chicken to serve.

Per serving: Cal 236, Net Carbs 2.3g, Fat 9g, Protein 18g

Cheesy Chicken with Cauliflower Steaks

Ingredients for 4 servings

4 slices chicken luncheon meat
1 large head cauliflower
½ tsp smoked paprika
2 tbsp olive oil
½ cup grated cheddar cheese
4 tbsp ranch dressing
2 tbsp chopped parsley
Salt and black pepper to taste

Directions and Total Time: approx. 30 minutes

Stand cauliflower on a flat surface and into 4 steaks from top to bottom. Season with paprika, salt, and pepper. and drizzle with olive oil. Heat a grill pan over medium heat and cook in the cauliflower on both sides until softened, 4 minutes. Top one side with chicken and sprinkle with cheddar cheese. Heat to melt the cheese. Drizzle with ranch dressing and garnish with parsley. Serve warm.

Per serving: Cal 253; Net Carbs 1g; Fat 22g; Protein 9g

Baked Chicken with Kale & Feta

Ingredients for 4 servings

4 chicken breasts, cut into strips
¼ cup shredded Monterey Jack cheese
2 tbsp olive oil
Salt and black pepper to taste
1 small onion, chopped
2 garlic cloves, minced
½ tbsp red wine vinegar
1 ½ crushed tomatoes
2 tbsp tomato paste
1 tsp Italian mixed herbs
2 medium zucchinis, chopped
1 cup baby kale
¼ cup crumbled feta cheese
½ cup grated Parmesan

Directions and Total Time: approx. 45 minutes

Preheat oven to 400 F. Heat olive oil in a skillet, season the chicken with salt and pepper, and cook for 8 minutes; set aside. Add in and sauté onion and garlic for 3 minutes. Mix in vinegar, tomatoes, and tomato paste. Cook for 8 minutes. Season with salt, pepper, and mixed herbs. Stir in chicken, zucchinis, kale, and feta cheese. Pour the mixture into a baking dish and top with Monterey Jack cheese. Bake for 15 minutes or until the cheese melts and is golden. Garnish with Parmesan cheese and serve.

Per serving: Cal 681; Net Carbs 6.6g; Fat 39g; Protein 69g

Buttered Roast Chicken

Ingredients for 6 servings

3 lb chicken, whole bird
8 tbsp butter, melted
1 large lemon, juiced
2 large lemons, thinly sliced

Directions and Total Time: approx. 1 hour 30 minutes

Preheat oven to 400 F. Put the chicken, breast side up in a baking dish. In a bowl, combine butter and lemon juice. Spread the mixture all over the chicken. Arrange lemon slices at the bottom of the dish and bake for 1 to 1 ½ hours. Baste the chicken with the juice every 20 minutes. Remove the chicken and serve with mashed turnips.

Per serving: Cal 393; Net Carbs 1g; Fat 22g; Protein 46g

Mushroom Chicken Cheeseburgers

Ingredients for 4 servings

4 large Portobello caps, destemmed
1 ½ lb ground chicken
Salt and black pepper to taste
1 tbsp tomato sauce
1 tbsp olive oil
6 slices Gruyere cheese
4 lettuce leaves
4 large tomato slices
¼ cup mayonnaise

Directions and Total Time: approx. 30 minutes

In a bowl, combine chicken, salt, pepper, and tomato sauce. Mold into 4 patties and set aside. Heat olive oil in a skillet; place in Portobello caps and cook for 3 minutes; set aside. Put the patties in the skillet and fry until brown and compacted, 8 minutes. Place Gruyere cheese slices on the patties, allow melting for 1 minute and lift each patty onto each mushroom cap. Divide the lettuce on top, then tomato slices, and top with some mayonnaise. Serve.

Per serving: Cal 510; Net Carbs 2.2g; Fat 34g; Protein 45g

Sweet Onion Chicken with Coconut Sauce

Ingredients for 6 servings

3 tbsp coconut oil
3 chicken breasts, halved
1 cup vegetable stock
2 sweet onions, sliced
1 lime, juiced
2 oz coconut cream
1 tsp red pepper flakes
1 tbsp fresh cilantro, chopped

Directions and Total Time: approx. 35 minutes

Cook the chicken in hot coconut oil, in a pan over medium heat for about 4-5 minutes; set aside. Place the sweet onions in the pan and cook for 4 minutes. Stir in vegetable stock, red pepper flakes, coconut cream, and lime juice. Return the chicken to the pan and cook covered for 15 minutes. Sprinkle with fresh cilantro and serve.

Per serving: Cal 481; Net Carbs 5.2g; Fat 27g; Protein 39g

Scallion & Saffron Chicken with Pasta

Ingredients for 4 servings

4 chicken breasts, cut into strips
1 cup shredded mozzarella
1 egg yolk
3 tbsp butter
½ tsp ground saffron threads
1 yellow onion, chopped
2 garlic cloves, minced
1 tbsp almond flour
1 pinch cardamom powder
1 pinch cinnamon powder
1 cup heavy cream
1 cup chicken stock
¼ cup chopped scallions
3 tbsp chopped parsley

Directions and Total Time: approx. 35 min + chilling time

Microwave mozzarella cheese for 2 minutes. Take out the bowl and allow cooling for 1 minute. Mix in egg yolk until well-combined. Lay a parchment paper on a flat surface, pour the cheese mixture on top and cover with another parchment paper. Flatten the dough into 1/8-inch thickness. Take off the parchment paper and cut the dough into thick fettuccine strands. Place in a bowl and refrigerate overnight. Bring 2 cups of water to a boil and add the keto fettuccine. Cook for 1 minute and drain; set aside. Melt butter in a skillet and cook the chicken for 5 minutes. Stir in saffron, onion, and garlic and cook until the onion softens, 3 minutes. Stir in almond flour, cardamom and cinnamon powders and cook for 1 minute.

Add in heavy cream and chicken stock and cook for 2-3 minutes. Mix in fettuccine and scallions. Garnish with parsley and serve warm.

Per serving: Cal 775; Net Carbs 3g; Fats 48g; Protein 73g

Beef

Easy Beef Burger Bake

Ingredients for 4 servings

¼ cup shredded Monterey Jack cheese
1 tbsp butter
1 lb ground beef
1 garlic clove, minced
1 red onion, chopped
2 tomatoes, chopped
1 tbsp dried basil
Salt and black pepper to taste
2 eggs
2 tbsp tomato paste
1 cup coconut cream

Directions and Total Time: approx. 35 minutes

Preheat oven to 400 F. Melt the butter in a large skillet over medium heat and add the beef. Cook for 6 minutes. Stir in garlic and onion and cook for another 3 minutes. Mix in tomatoes, basil, salt, and pepper until the tomatoes soften. Add 2/3 of Monterey Jack cheese and stir to melt. In a bowl, crack the eggs and whisk with tomato paste, salt, and coconut cream. Spoon the beef mixture into a greased baking sheet and spread the egg mixture on top. Sprinkle with the remaining cheese and bake for 20 minutes. Serve.

Per serving: Cal 469; Net Carbs 4.5g; Fat 34g; Protein 33g

Cheesy Tomato Beef Tart

Ingredients for 4 servings

2 tbsp olive oil
1 small brown onion, chopped
1 garlic clove, finely chopped
1 lb ground beef
1 tbsp Italian mixed herbs
4 tbsp tomato paste
4 tbsp coconut flour
¾ cup almond flour
4 tbsp flaxseeds
1 tsp baking powder
3 tbsp coconut oil, melted
1 egg
¼ cup ricotta, crumbled
¼ cup cheddar, shredded

Directions and Total Time: approx. 1 hour 30 minutes

Preheat oven to 350 F. Line a pie dish with parchment paper. Heat olive oil in a large skillet over medium heat and sauté onion and garlic until softened, 3 minutes.

Add in beef and cook until brown. Season with herbs and stir in tomato paste and ½ cup water; reduce the heat to low. Simmer for 20 minutes; set aside.

In a food processor, add the flours, flaxseeds, baking powder, coconut oil, egg, and 4 tbsp water. Mix starting on low speed to medium until evenly combined and dough is formed. Spread the dough in the pie pan and bake for 12 minutes. Remove and spread the meat filling on top. Scatter with ricotta and cheddar cheeses. Bake until the cheeses melt and are golden brown on top, 35 minutes. Remove the pie, let cool for 3 minutes, slice, and serve with green salad and garlic vinaigrette.

Per serving: Cal 603; Net Carbs 2.3g; Fat 39g; Protein 57g

Awesome Beef Stuffed Zucchini

Ingredients for 4 servings4

2 zucchinis
2 tbsp butter
1 lb ground beef
1 red bell pepper, chopped
2 garlic cloves, minced
1 shallot, finely chopped
2 tbsp taco seasoning
½ cup finely chopped parsley
1 tbsp olive oil
1¼ cups shredded cheddar

Directions and Total Time: approx. 50 minutes

Preheat oven to 400 F. Grease a baking sheet with cooking spray. Using a knife, cut zucchinis into halves and scoop out the pulp; set aside. Chop the flesh. Melt the butter in a skillet over medium heat and cook the beef until brown, frequently stirring and breaking the lumps, 10 minutes. Stir in bell pepper, zucchini pulp, garlic, shallot, taco seasoning and cook until softened, 5 minutes. Place the boats on the baking sheet with the open side up. Spoon in the beef mixture, divide the parsley on top, drizzle with olive oil, and top with cheddar cheese. Bake for 20 minutes until the cheese melts and is golden brown on top. Serve warm with tangy lettuce salad.

Per serving: Cal 423; Net Carbs 2.9g; Fat 29g; Protein 35g

Pesto Beef Casserole with Goat Cheese

Ingredients for 4 servings

2 tbsp ghee
1 ½ lb ground beef
Salt and black pepper to taste
3 oz pitted green olives
5 oz goat cheese, crumbled
1 garlic clove, minced
3 oz basil pesto
1¼ cups coconut cream

Directions and Total Time: approx. 45 minutes

Preheat oven to 400 F. Grease a casserole dish with cooking spray. Melt ghee in a deep skillet and cook the beef until brown; stirring frequently. Season with salt and pepper. Spoon and spread the beef at the bottom of the casserole dish. Top with olives, goat cheese, and garlic. In a bowl, mix pesto and coconut cream and pour the mixture all over the beef. Bake until lightly brown around the edges and bubbly, 25 minutes. Serve with a leafy green salad.

Per serving: Cal 656; Net Carbs 4g; Fat 51g; Protein 47g

Maple Jalapeño Beef Plate

Ingredients for 4 servings

1 lb ribeye steak, sliced into ¼-inch strips
2 tsp sugar-free maple syrup
Salt and black pepper to taste
1 tbsp coconut flour
½ tsp xanthan gum
2 tbsp olive oil
1 tbsp coconut oil
1 tsp freshly pureed ginger
1 clove garlic, minced
1 red chili, minced
4 tbsp tamari sauce
1 tsp sesame oil
1 tsp fish sauce
2 tbsp white wine vinegar
1 tsp hot sauce
1 small bok choy, quartered
½ jalapeño, sliced into rings
1 tbsp toasted sesame seeds
1 scallion, chopped

Directions and Total Time: approx. 40 minutes

Season the beef with salt and pepper and rub with coconut flour and
xanthan gum; set aside. Heat olive oil in a skillet and fry the beef until
brown on all sides. Heat coconut oil in a wok and sauté ginger, garlic,
red chili, and bok choy for 5 minutes. Mix in tamari sauce, sesame oil,

fish sauce, vinegar, hot sauce, and maple syrup; cook for 2 minutes. Add the beef and cook for 2 minutes. Spoon into bowls, top with jalapeño pepper, scallion and sesame seeds. Serve.

Per serving: Cal 507; Net Carbs 2.9g; Fat 43g; Protein 25g

Cheese & Beef Avocado Boats

Ingredients for 4 servings

2 tbsp avocado oil
1 lb ground beef
Salt and black pepper to taste
1 tsp onion powder
1 tsp cumin powder
1 tsp garlic powder
2 tsp taco seasoning
2 tsp smoked paprika
1 cup raw pecans, chopped
1 tbsp hemp seeds, hulled
7 tbsp shredded Monterey Jack
2 avocados, halved and pitted
1 medium tomato, sliced
¼ cup shredded iceberg lettuce
4 tbsp sour cream
4 tbsp shredded Monterey Jack

Directions and Total Time: approx. 30 minutes

Heat half of avocado oil in a skillet and cook beef for 10 minutes. Season with salt, pepper, onion powder, cumin, garlic, taco seasoning, and smoked paprika. Add the pecans and hemp seeds and stir-fry for 10 minutes. Fold in 3 tbsp Monterey Jack cheese to melt. Spoon the filling into avocado holes, top with 1-2 slices of tomatoes, some lettuce, 1 tbsp each of sour cream, and the remaining Monterey Jack cheese and serve immediately.

Per serving: Cal 840; Net Carbs 4g; Fat 70g; Protein 42g

Celery & Beef Stuffed Mushrooms

Ingredients for 4 servings

½ cup shredded Pecorino Romano cheese
2 tbsp olive oil
½ celery stalk, chopped
1 shallot, finely chopped
1 lb ground beef
2 tbsp mayonnaise
1 tsp Old Bay seasoning
½ tsp garlic powder
2 large eggs
4 caps Portobello mushrooms
1 tbsp flaxseed meal
2 tbsp shredded Parmesan
1 tbsp chopped parsley

Directions and Total Time: approx. 55 minutes

Preheat oven to 350 F. Heat olive oil in a skillet and sauté celery and shallot for 3 minutes; set aside. Add beef to the skillet and cook for 10 minutes; add to the shallot mixture. Pour in mayonnaise, Old Bay seasoning, garlic powder, Pecorino cheese and crack in the eggs. Combine the mixture evenly. Arrange the mushrooms on a greased baking sheet and fill with the meat mixture. Combine flaxseed meal and Parmesan cheese in a bowl and sprinkle over the mushroom filling. Bake until the cheese melts, 30 minutes. Garnish with parsley to serve.

Per serving: Cal 375; Net Carbs 3.5g; Fat 22g; Protein 37g

Shiitake Butter Steak

Ingredients for 4 servings

2 cups shiitake mushrooms, sliced
4 ribeye steaks
2 tbsp butter
2 tsp olive oil
Salt and black pepper to taste

Directions and Total Time: approx. 25 minutes

Heat olive oil in a pan over medium heat. Rub the steaks with salt and pepper and cook for 4 minutes per side; reserve. Melt butter in the pan and sauté shiitakes for 6 minutes. Pour the mushrooms over the steaks and serve.

Per serving: Cal 370; Net Carbs 3g; Fat 31g; Protein 33g

Pork

Tuscan Pork Tenderloin with Cauli Rice

Ingredients for 4 servings

1 cup loosely packed fresh baby spinach
2 tbsp olive oil
1 ½ lb pork tenderloin, cubed
Salt and black pepper to taste
½ tsp cumin powder
2 cups cauliflower rice
½ cup water
1 cup grape tomatoes, halved
3/4 cup crumbled feta cheese

Directions and Total Time: approx. 30 minutes

Heat olive oil in a skillet, season the pork with salt, pepper, and cumin and sear on both sides for 5 minutes until brown. Stir in cauli rice and pour in water. Cook for 5 minutes or until cauliflower softens. Mix in spinach to wilt, 1 minute and add the tomatoes. Spoon into bowls, sprinkle with feta cheese, and serve with hot sauce.

Per serving: Cal 377; Net Carbs 1.9g; Fat 17g; Protein 43g

Mushroom &Pork Casserole

Ingredients for 4 servings

1 cup portobello mushrooms, chopped
1 cup ricotta, crumbled
1 cup Italian cheese blend
4 carrots, thinly sliced
Salt and black pepper to taste
1 clove garlic, minced
1 ¼ pounds ground pork
4 green onions, chopped
15 oz canned tomatoes
4 tbsp pork rinds, crushed
¼ cup chopped parsley
3 tbsp olive oil
⅓ cup water

Directions and Total Time: approx. 38 minutes

Mix parsley, ricotta cheese, and Italian cheese blend in a bowl; set aside. Heat olive oil in a skillet and cook the ground pork for 3 minutes. Add in garlic, half of the green onions, mushrooms, and 2 tbsp of pork rinds. Continue cooking for 3 minutes. Stir in tomatoes and water and cook for 3 minutes. Sprinkle a baking dish with 2 tbsp of pork rinds, top with half of the carrots and salt, 2/3 of the pork mixture, and the cheese mixture. Repeat the layering process a second time to exhaust the ingredients. Cover the baking dish with foil and bake for 20 minutes at 370 F.

Remove the foil and brown the top of the casserole with the broiler side of the oven for 2 minutes. Serve warm.

Per serving: Cal 672; Net Carbs 7.9g; Fat 56g; Protein 35g

Barbecue Baked Pork Chops

Ingredients for 4 servings

½ cup grated flaxseed meal
1 tsp dried thyme
1 tsp paprika
Salt and black pepper to taste
¼ tsp chili powder
1 ½ tsp garlic powder
1 tbsp dried parsley
1/2 tsp onion powder
1/8 tsp basil
4 pork chops
1 tbsp melted butter
½ cup BBQ sauce

Directions and Total Time: approx. 60 min + chilling time

Preheat oven to 400 F. In a bowl, mix flaxseed meal, thyme, paprika, salt, pepper, chili, garlic powder, parsley, onion powder, and basil. Rub the pork chops with the mixture. Melt butter in a skillet and sear pork on both sides, 8 minutes. Transfer to a greased baking sheet, brush with BBQ sauce, and bake for 50 minutes. Allow resting for 10 minutes, slice, and serve with buttered parsnips.

Per serving: Cal 385; Net Carbs 1.6g; Fat 19g; Protein 44g

Celery Braised Pork Shanks in Wine Sauce

Ingredients for 4 servings

3 tbsp olive oil
3 lb pork shanks
3 celery stalks, chopped
5 garlic cloves, minced
1 ½ cups crushed tomatoes
½ cup red wine
¼ tsp red chili flakes
¼ cup chopped parsley

Directions and Total Time: approx. 2 hours 30 minutes

Preheat oven to 300 F. Heat olive oil in a saucepan and brown pork on all sides for 4 minutes; set aside. Add in celery and garlic and sauté for 3 minutes. Return the pork.Top with tomatoes, red wine, and red chili flakes. Cover the lid and put the saucepan in the oven. Cook for 2 hours, turning the meat every 30 minutes. In the last 15 minutes, open the lid and increase the temperature to 450 F. Take out the pot, stir in parsley, and serve the meat with sauce on a bed of creamy mashed cauliflower.

Per serving: Cal 520; Net Carbs 1.4g; Fat 20g; Protein 75g

Dijon Pork Loin Roast

Ingredients for 6 servings

3 lb boneless pork loin roast
5 cloves garlic, minced
Salt and black pepper to taste
1 tbsp Dijon mustard
1 tsp dried basil
2 tsp olive oil

Directions and Total Time: approx. 30 min + chilling time

Preheat oven to 400 F. Place the pork loin in a greased baking dish. In a bowl, mix garlic, salt, pepper, Dijon mustard, and basil. Rub the mixture onto the pork. Drizzle with olive oil and bake for 15 minutes or until cooked within and brown outside. Transfer to a flat surface and let cool for 5 minutes. Slice the pork and sliced.

Per serving: Cal 311; Net Carbs 2g; Fat 9g; Protein 51g

Juicy Pork Chops with Raspberries

Ingredients for 4 servings

1 lb pork tenderloin, cut into ½-inch medallions
2 cups fresh raspberries
¼ cup water
1 tsp chicken bouillon granules
½ cup almond flour
2 large eggs, lightly beaten
2/3 cup grated Parmesan
Salt and black pepper to taste
6 tbsp butter, divided
1 tsp minced garlic
Sliced fresh raspberries

Directions and Total Time: approx. 30 minutes

To a blender, add raspberries, water, and chicken granules; process until smooth and set aside. In two separate bowls, pour almond flour and Parmesan cheese. Season the meat with salt and pepper. Coat in the almond flour, then in the eggs, and finally in the cheese.

Melt 2 tbsp of butter in a skillet and fry the pork for 3 minutes per side or until the meat cooks within. Transfer to a plate and cover to keep warm. In the same skillet, melt remaining butter and sauté garlic for 1 minute. Stir in raspberry mixture and cook for 3 minutes. Spoon sauce on top of the pork. Garnish with raspberries and serve.

Per serving: Cal 488; Net Carbs 6.1g; Fat 23g; Protein 34g

Cheesy Sausages in Creamy Onion Sauce

Ingredients for 4 servings

2 tsp almond flour
1 (16 oz) pork sausages
6 tbsp golden flaxseed meal
1 egg, beaten
1 tbsp olive oil
8 oz cream cheese, softened
3 tbsp freshly chopped chives
3 tsp freshly pureed onion
3 tbsp chicken broth
2 tbsp almond milk

Directions and Total Time: approx. 30 minutes

Prick the sausages with a fork all around, roll in the almond flour, dip in the egg, and then in the flaxseed meal. Heat olive oil in a skillet and fry sausages until brown, 15 minutes. Transfer to a plate. In a saucepan, combine cream cheese, chives, onion, chicken broth, and almond milk. Cook and stir over medium heat until smooth and evenly mixed, 5 minutes. Plate the sausages and spoon the sauce on top. Serve immediately with steamed broccoli.

Per serving: Cal 461; Net Carbs 0.5g; Fat 32g; Protein 34g

Sweet Pork Chops with Brie Cheese

Ingredients for 4 servings

3 tbsp olive oil
2 large red onions, sliced
2 tbsp balsamic vinegar
1 tsp maple (sugar-free) syrup
Salt and black pepper to taste
4 pork chops
4 slices brie cheese
2 tbsp chopped mint leaves

Directions and Total Time: approx. 45 minutes

Heat 1 tbsp olive oil in a skillet until smoky. Reduce to low and sauté onions until brown. Pour in vinegar, maple syrup, and salt. Cook with frequent stirring to prevent burning until the onions caramelize, 15 minutes; set aside. Heat the remaining olive oil in the same skillet, season the pork with salt and black pepper, and cook for 12 minutes. Put a brie slice on each meat and top with the caramelized onions; let the cheese to melt for 2 minutes. Spoon the meat with the topping onto plates and garnish with mint.

Per serving: Cal 457; Net Carbs 3.1g; Fat 25g; Protein 46g

Seafood

Tuna Salad Pickle Boats

Ingredients for 12 servings

18 oz canned and drained tuna
6 large dill pickles
¼ tsp garlic powder
¼ cup sugar-free mayonnaise
1 tsp onion powder

Directions and Total Time: approx. 40 minutes

Mix the mayo, tuna, onion and garlic powders in a bowl. Cut the pickles in half, lengthwise. Top each half with tuna mixture. Place in the fridge for 30 minutes and serve.

Per serving: Cal 118; Net Carbs 1.5g; Fat 10g; Protein 11g

Tuna Stuffed Avocado

Ingredients for 4 servings

2 avocados, halved and pitted
4 oz Colby Jack, grated
2 oz canned tuna, flaked
2 tbsp chives, chopped
Salt and black pepper, to taste
½ cup curly endive, chopped

Directions and Total Time: approx. 20 minutes

Preheat oven to 360 F. Set avocado halves in an ovenproof dish. In a bowl, mix colby Jack cheese, chives, pepper, salt, and tuna. Stuff the cheese/tuna mixture in avocado halves. Bake for 15 minutes or until the top is golden brown. Serve with curly endive.

Per serving: Cal: 286; Net Carbs 9g; Fat 23.9g; Protein 11g

Tuna & Zucchini Traybake

Ingredients for 4 servings

1 bunch asparagus, trimmed and cut into 1-inch pieces
1 (15 oz) can tuna in water, drained and flaked
1 tbsp butter
1 cup green beans, chopped
2 tbsp arrowroot starch
2 cups coconut milk
4 zucchinis, spiralized
1 cup grated Parmesan cheese

Directions and Total Time: approx. 40 minutes

Preheat the oven to 380 F. Melt butter in a skillet and sauté green beans and asparagus until softened, about 5 minutes; set aside. In a saucepan over medium heat, mix in arrowroot starch with coconut milk. Bring to a boil and cook with frequent stirring until thickened, 3 minutes. Stir in half of the Parmesan cheese until melted. Mix in the green beans, asparagus, zucchinis, and tuna. Transfer the mixture to a baking dish and cover with the remaining Parmesan cheese. Bake until the cheese is melted and golden, about 20 minutes. Serve warm.

Per serving: Cal 389; Net Carbs 8g; Fats 34g; Protein 11g

Bacon Zoodles with Sardines

Ingredients for 2 servings

½ cup canned diced tomatoes
4 cups zoodles
2 oz cubed bacon
4 oz canned sardines, chopped
21 tbsp sardine oil
1 tbsp capers
1 tbsp parsley
1 tsp minced garlic

Directions and Total Time: approx. 10 minutes

Warm the sardine oil in a pan over medium heat. Add in garlic and cook for 1 minute. Add the bacon and cook for 2 minutes. Stir in the tomatoes and let simmer for 5 minutes. Add zoodles and sardines and cook for 3 minutes. Serve.

Per serving: Cal 230; Net Carbs 6g; Fat 31g; Protein 20g

Vegan and vegetarian

One-Pot Spicy Brussel Sprouts with Carrots

Ingredients for 4 servings

1 lb Brussels sprouts
¼ cup olive oil
4 green onions, chopped
2 carrots, grated
Salt and black pepper to taste
Hot chili sauce

Directions and Total Time: approx. 15 minutes

Sauté green onions in warm olive oil for 2 minutes. Sprinkle with salt and pepper and transfer to a plate. Trim the Brussel sprouts and cut in halves. Leave the small ones as wholes. Pour the Brussel sprouts with and carrots into the same saucepan and stir-fry until softened but al dente. Season to taste and stir in onions. Cook for 3 minutes. Top with the hot chili sauce and serve.

Per serving: Cal 198; Net Carbs 6.5g; Fat 14g; Protein 4.9g

Zucchini-Cranberry Cake Squares

Ingredients for 6 servings

1 ¼ cups chopped zucchinis
2 tbsp olive oil
½ cup dried cranberries
1 lemon, zested
3 eggs
1 ½ cups almond flour
½ tsp baking powder
1 tsp cinnamon powder
A pinch of salt

Directions and Total Time: approx. 45 minutes

Preheat oven to 350 F. Line a square cake tin with parchment paper. Combine zucchinis, olive oil, cranberries, lemon zest, and eggs in a bowl until evenly combined. Add almond flour, baking powder, cinnamon powder, and salt into the mixture. Pour the mixture into the cake tin and bake for 30 minutes. Remove, allow cooling in the tin for 10 minutes, and transfer the cake to a wire rack to cool completely. Cut into squares and serve.

Per serving: Cal 121; Net Carbs 2.5g, Fat 10g, Protein 4g

Egg Cauli Fried Rice with Grilled Cheese

Ingredients for 4 servings

2 cups cauliflower rice, steamed
½ lb halloumi, cut into ¼ to ½ inch slabs
1 tbsp ghee
4 eggs, beaten
1 green bell pepper, chopped
¼ cup green beans, chopped
1 tsp soy sauce
2 tbsp chopped parsley

Directions and Total Time: approx. 10 minutes

Melt ghee in a skillet and pour in the eggs. Swirl the pan to spread the eggs around and cook for 1 minute. Move the scrambled eggs to the side of the skillet, add bell pepper and green beans, and sauté for 3 minutes. Pour in the cauli rice and cook for 2 minutes. Top with soy sauce; combine evenly, and cook for 2 minutes. Dish into plates, garnish with the parsley, and set aside. Preheat a grill pan and grill halloumi cheese on both sides until the cheese lightly browns. Place on the side of the rice and serve warm.

Per serving: Cal 275; Net Carbs 4.5g, Fat 19g, Protein 15g

Fake Mushroom Risotto

Ingredients for 4 servings

2 shallots, diced
3 tbsp olive oil
¼ cup vegetable broth
⅓ cup Parmesan cheese
4 tbsp butter
3 tbsp chopped chives
2 pounds mushrooms, sliced
4 ½ cups riced cauliflower

Directions and Total Time: approx. 15 minutes

Heat 2 tbsp oil in a saucepan. Add the mushrooms and cook over medium heat for 3 minutes. Remove and set aside. Heat the remaining oil and cook the shallots for 2 minutes. Stir in the cauliflower and broth and cook until the liquid is absorbed. Stir in the rest of the ingredients.

Per serving: Cal 264; Net Carbs 8.4g; Fat 18g; Protein 11g

Cheesy Eggplant Pizza

Ingredients for 2 servings

6 oz mozzarella, grated
2 tbsp cream cheese
2 tbsp Parmesan cheese
1 tsp oregano
½ cup almond flour
2 tbsp psyllium husk
4 oz grated cheddar cheese
¼ cup marinara sauce
⅔ eggplant, sliced
1 tomato, sliced
2 tbsp chopped basil
6 black olives

Directions and Total Time: approx. 40 minutes

Preheat the oven to 400 F. Melt mozzarella cheese in the microwave. Combine cream cheese, Parmesan cheese, oregano, almond flour, and psyllium husk in a bowl. Stir in the melted mozzarella cheese and mix to combine. Divide the dough in 2. Roll out the crusts in circles and place on a lined baking sheet. Bake for 10 minutes. Top with cheddar cheese, marinara, eggplant, tomato, and basil. Return to oven and bake for 10 minutes. Serve with olives.

Per serving: Cal 510; Net Carbs 3.7g; Fat 39g; Protein 31g

Eggplant & Goat Cheese Pizza

Ingredients for 4 servings

4 tbsp olive oil
2 eggplants, sliced lengthwise
1 cup tomato sauce
2 garlic cloves, minced
1 red onion, sliced
12 oz goat cheese, crumbled
Salt and black pepper to taste
½ tsp cinnamon powder
1 cup mozzarella, shredded
2 tbsp oregano, chopped

Directions and Total Time: approx. 45 minutes

Line a baking sheet with parchment paper. Lay the eggplant slices in a baking dish and drizzle with some olive oil. Bake for 20 minutes at 390 F. Heat the remaining olive oil in a skillet and sauté garlic and onion for 3 minutes. Stir in goat cheese and tomato sauce and season with salt and pepper. Simmer for 10 minutes. Remove eggplant from the oven and spread the cheese sauce on top. Sprinkle with mozzarella cheese and oregano. Bake further for 10 minutes until the cheese melts. Slice and serve.

Per serving: Cal 557; Net Carbs 8.3g; Fat 44g; Protein 33g

Mushroom & Broccoli Pizza

Ingredients for 4 servings

½ cup almond flour
¼ tsp salt
2 tbsp ground psyllium husk
2 tbsp olive oil
1 cup sliced fresh mushrooms
1 white onion, thinly sliced
3 cups broccoli florets
2 garlic cloves, minced
½ cup sugar-free pizza sauce
4 tomatoes, sliced
1 ½ cups grated mozzarella
⅓ cup grated Parmesan

Directions and Total Time: approx. 25 minutes

Preheat oven to 390 F. Line a baking sheet with parchment paper. In a bowl, mix almond flour, salt, psyllium powder, 1 tbsp of olive oil, and 1 cup of lukewarm water until dough forms. Spread the mixture on the pizza pan and bake for 10 minutes. Heat the remaining olive oil in a skillet and sauté mushrooms, onion, garlic, and broccoli for 5 minutes. Spread the pizza sauce on the crust and top with the broccoli mixture, tomato, and mozzarella and Parmesan cheeses. Bake for 5 minutes. Serve sliced.

Per serving: Cal 180; Net Carbs 3.6g; Fats 9g; Protein 17g

Snacks and side dish

Parmesan Green Bean Crisps

Ingredients for 6 servings

¼ cup Parmesan, shredded
¼ cup pork rind crumbs
1 tsp minced garlic
2 eggs
1 lb green beans
Salt and black pepper to taste

Directions and Total Time: approx. 30 minutes

Preheat oven to 425 F. Line a baking sheet with foil. Mix Parmesan cheese, pork rinds, garlic, salt, and pepper in a bowl. Beat the eggs in another bowl. Coat green beans in eggs, then in the cheese mixture, and arrange them evenly on the baking sheet. Grease lightly with cooking spray and bake for 15 minutes. Transfer to a wire rack to cool. Serve.

Per serving: Cal 210; Net Carbs 3g; Fat 19g; Protein 5g

Cheese & Garlic Crackers

Ingredients for 6 servings

1 ¼ cups Pecorino Romano cheese, grated
1 ¼ cups coconut flour
Salt and black pepper to taste
1 tsp garlic powder
¼ cup ghee, softened
¼ tsp sweet paprika
½ cup heavy cream

Directions and Total Time: approx. 30 minutes

Preheat oven to 350 F. Mix coconut flour, Pecorino Romano cheese, salt, pepper, garlic, and paprika in a bowl. Add in ghee and mix well. Top with heavy cream and mix again until a thick mixture has formed. Cover the dough with plastic wrap. Use a rolling pin to spread out the dough into a light rectangle. Cut into cracker squares and arrange them on a baking sheet. Bake for 20 minutes.

Per serving: Cal 115; Net Carbs 0.7g; Fat 3g; Protein 5g

Spinach & Cheese Puff Balls

Ingredients for 4 servings

¼ cup crumbled ricotta
¼ tsp nutmeg
¼ tsp black pepper
2 tbsp heavy cream
¼ tsp garlic powder
¼ tsp onion powder
1 tbsp butter, melted
3 tbsp Parmesan cheese
1 egg
4 oz spinach
½ cup almond flour

Directions and Total Time: approx. 30 minutes

Place all ingredients in a food processor. Process until smooth. Place in the freezer for 10 minutes. Make balls out of the mixture and arrange them on a lined baking sheet. Bake in the oven at 350 F for 10-12 minutes. Serve.

Per serving: Cal 60; Net Carbs 0.8g; Fat 5g; Protein 8g

Savory Lime Fried Artichokes

Ingredients for 4 servings

12 fresh baby artichokes
2 tbsp lime juice
2 tbsp olive oil
Salt to taste

Directions and Total Time: approx. 20 minutes

Slice artichokes vertically into narrow wedges. Drain on paper towels before frying. Heat olive oil in a skillet over medium heat and fry the artichokes until browned and crispy. Sprinkle with lime juice and serve.

Per serving: Cal 35; Net Carbs: 2.9g; Fat: 2.4g; Protein: 2g

Cheesy Chicken Wraps

Ingredients for 4 servings

¼ tsp garlic powder
4 oz fontina cheese
4 raw chicken tenders
4 prosciutto slices

Directions and Total Time: approx. 20 minutes

Pound chicken until half an inch thick. Season with garlic powder. Cut fontina cheese into 8 strips. Place a slice of prosciutto on a flat surface. Place a chicken tender on top. Top with a fontina strip. Roll the chicken and secure with skewers. Grill the wraps for 3 minutes per side. Serve.

Per serving: Cal 174; Net Carbs: 1g; Fat: 10g; Protein: 17g

Brussel Sprout & Bacon Wraps

Ingredients for 4 servings

16 Brussel sprouts, trimmed
8 bacon slices
1/8 teaspoon chili pepper

Directions and Total Time: approx. 15 minutes

Preheat oven to 420 F. Line a baking sheet with parchment paper. Cut the bacon slices in half. Wrap each Brussels sprout with a bacon strip. Transfer the wraps to the baking sheet and bake in the oven for 25-30 until crispy. Sprinkle with chili powder and serve immediately.

Per serving: Cal 193; Net Carbs 1.6g; Fat 14g; Protein 12g

Gruyere & Ham Waffle Sandwiches

Ingredients for 4 servings

4 slices smoked ham, chopped
4 tbsp butter, softened
½ cup Gruyère cheese, grated
6 eggs
½ tsp baking powder
½ tsp dried thyme
4 tomato slices

Directions and Total Time: approx. 20 minutes

In a bowl, mix eggs, baking powder, thyme, and butter. Set a waffle iron over medium heat, add in ¼ cup of the batter and cook for 6 minutes until golden. Do the same with the remaining batter until you have 8 thin waffles. Lay a tomato slice on top of a waffle, followed by a ham slice, then top with ¼ of the grated cheese. Cover with another waffle, place the sandwich in the waffle iron and cook until the cheese melts. Repeat with the remaining ingredients.

Per serving: Cal 276; Net Carbs 3.1g; Fat 22g; Protein 16g

Dessert

Gingerbread Cheesecake

Ingredients for 6 servings

For the crust:
1 ¾ cups golden flaxseed meal
6 tbsp melted butter
¼ swerve sugar
A pinch of salt

For the filling
8 oz cream cheese, softened
¾ cup swerve sugar
¼ cup sugar-free maple syrup
3 large eggs
¼ cup sour cream
2 tbsp almond flour
1 tsp pure vanilla extract
2 tsp smooth ginger paste
1 tsp cinnamon powder
¼ tsp nutmeg powder
¼ tsp salt
A pinch of cloves powder

Directions and Total Time: approx. 1 hour 45 minutes

Preheat oven to 325 F. In a bowl, mix flaxseed meal, butter, swerve, and salt. Pour and fit the mixture into a greased pan using a spoon. Bake the crust for 15 minutes or until firm. In a bowl, using an electric mixer, beat cream cheese, swerve sugar, and maple syrup until smooth. Whisk in one after the other, the eggs, sour cream, almond flour, vanilla extract, ginger paste, cinnamon, nutmeg, salt, and clove powder. Pour the mixture onto the crust while shaking to release any bubbles. Cover with foil and bake for 55 minutes until the center of the cake jiggles slightly. Remove the cake, let cool, and release the cake pan. Garnish with ginger powder, slice, and serve.

Per serving: Cal 682; Net Carbs 4.3g; Fat 49g; Protein 31g

Vanilla Berry Mug Cakes

Ingredients for 4 servings

1 tbsp butter, melted
2 tbsp cream cheese
2 tbsp coconut flour
1 tbsp xylitol
1 tsp vanilla extract
¼ tsp baking powder
1 medium egg
6 mixed berries, mashed

Directions and Total Time: approx. 5 minutes

In a bowl, whisk butter, cream cheese, coconut flour, xylitol, baking powder, egg, and mashed berries. Pour the mixture into two mugs and microwave for 80 seconds or until set. Let cool for 1 minute and enjoy.

Per serving: Cal 98; Net Carbs 2.4g; Fat 4g; Protein 3.5g

Keto Fat Bombs

Ingredients for 4 servings

½ cup peanut butter
½ cup coconut oil
4 tbsp cocoa powder
½ cup erythritol

Directions and Total Time: approx. 3 min + cooling time

Melt butter and coconut oil in the microwave for 45 seconds, stirring twice until properly melted. Mix in cocoa powder and erythritol until completely combined. Pour into muffin molds and refrigerate for 3 hours to harden.

Per serving: Cal 193; Net Carbs 2g; Fat 18.3g; Protein 4g

Heart-Shaped Red Velvet Cakes

Ingredients for 6 servings

½ cup butter
6 eggs
1 tsp vanilla extract
1 cup Greek yogurt
1 cup swerve sugar
1 cup almond flour
½ cup coconut flour
2 tbsp cocoa powder
2 tbsp baking powder
¼ tsp salt
1 tbsp red food coloring

For the frosting:
1 cup mascarpone cheese
½ cup erythritol
1 tsp vanilla extract
2 tbsp heavy cream

Directions and Total Time: approx. 30 minutes

Preheat oven to 400 F. Grease 2 heart-shaped cake pans with butter. In a bowl, beat butter, eggs, vanilla, Greek yogurt, and swerve sugar until smooth. In another bowl, mix the almond and coconut flours, cocoa, salt, baking powder, and red food coloring. Combine both mixtures until smooth and divide the batter between the two cake pans. Bake in the oven for 25 minutes or until a toothpick inserted comes out clean. In a bowl, using an electric mixer, whisk the mascarpone cheese and erythritol until smooth. Mix in vanilla and heavy cream. Transfer to a wire rack, let cool, and spread the frosting on top. Serve.

Per serving: Cal 643; Net Carbs 9.2g; Fat 46g; Protein 37g

Sticky Maple Cinnamon Cake

Ingredients for 4 servings

9 tbsp butter, melted and cooled
½ cup sugar-free maple syrup + extra for topping
6 eggs
2 tsp cream cheese, softened
1 tsp vanilla extract
2 tbsp heavy cream
¼ cup almond flour
1 ½ tsp baking powder
1 tsp cinnamon powder
½ tsp salt

Directions and Total Time: approx. 30 minutes

Preheat oven to 400 F. Grease a cake pan with melted butter. In a bowl, beat the eggs, butter, cream cheese, vanilla, heavy cream, and maple syrup until smooth. In another bowl, mix almond flour, baking powder, cinnamon, and salt. Combine both mixtures until smooth and pour the batter into the cake pan. Bake for 25 minutes or until a toothpick inserted comes out clean. Transfer the cake to a wire rack to cool and drizzle with maple syrup.

Per serving: Cal 362; Net Carbs 1.5g; Fat 35g; Protein 8.9g

Keto Caramel Cake

Ingredients for 4 servings

½ cup sugar-free caramel sauce + extra for topping
2 ½ cups almond flour
¼ cup coconut flour
¼ cup whey protein powder
1 tbsp baking powder
½ tsp salt
1 cup erythritol
4 large eggs
1 tsp vanilla extract
1 cup almond milk

Directions and Total Time: approx. 30 minutes

Preheat oven to 400 F. In a bowl, mix almond and coconut flours, protein and baking powders, and salt. In another bowl, mix erythritol, eggs, vanilla, almond milk, and ½ cup of caramel sauce. Combine both mixtures until smooth batter forms. Pour batter into a greased pan; bake for 22 minutes. Cool and top with caramel sauce to serve.

Per serving: Cal 313; Net Carbs 3.4g; Fat 29g; Protein 8.2g

Tasty Hot Chocolate with Peanuts

Ingredients for 4 servings

3 cups almond milk
4 tbsp cocoa powder
2 tbsp swerve
3 tbsp peanut butter
Chopped peanuts to garnish

Directions and Total Time: approx. 10 minutes

In a saucepan, add the almond milk, cocoa powder, and swerve. Stir the mixture until the swerve dissolves. Set the pan over low to heat through for 5 minutes, without boiling. Swirl the mix occasionally. Turn the heat off and stir in the peanut butter until incorporated. Pour the hot chocolate into mugs and sprinkle with chopped peanuts.

Per serving: Cal 225; Net Carbs 0.8g; Fat 22g; Protein 4.5g

Chocolate Crunch Bars

Ingredients for 4 servings

1 ½ cups chocolate chips
¼ cup almond butter
½ cup sugar-free maple syrup
¼ cup melted butter
1 tbsp sesame seeds
1 cup chopped walnuts

Directions and Total Time: approx. 5 min + chilling time

Line a baking sheet with parchment paper. In a bowl, mix chocolate chips, almond butter, maple syrup, butter, seeds, and walnuts. Spread the mixture onto the sheet and refrigerate until firm, about 1 hour. Cut into bars to serve.

Per serving: Cal 713; Net Carbs 7.1g; Fat 75g; Protein 7.9g

Cream Cheese Cookies

Ingredients for 4 servings

¼ cup softened butter
2 oz softened cream cheese
1/3 cup xylitol
1 large egg
2 tsp vanilla extract
¼ tsp salt
1 tbsp sour cream
3 cups blanched almond flour

Directions and Total Time: approx. 25 minutes

Preheat oven to 350 F. Line a baking sheet with parchment paper. In a bowl, using an electric mixer, whisk butter, cream cheese, and xylitol until fluffy and light in color. Beat in egg, vanilla, salt, and sour cream until smooth. Add in flour and mix until smooth batter forms. With a cookie scoop, arrange 1 ½ tbsp of batter onto the sheet at 2-inch intervals. Bake for 15 minutes until lightly golden.

Per serving: Cal 177; Net Carbs 1.3g; Fat 17g; Protein 3g